August 2020 Edition

THE ART OF FINDING ISAIAH
イザヤを見つける術

THE COLORING BOOK

Written &
Illustrated by
Felicia Guy-Lynch

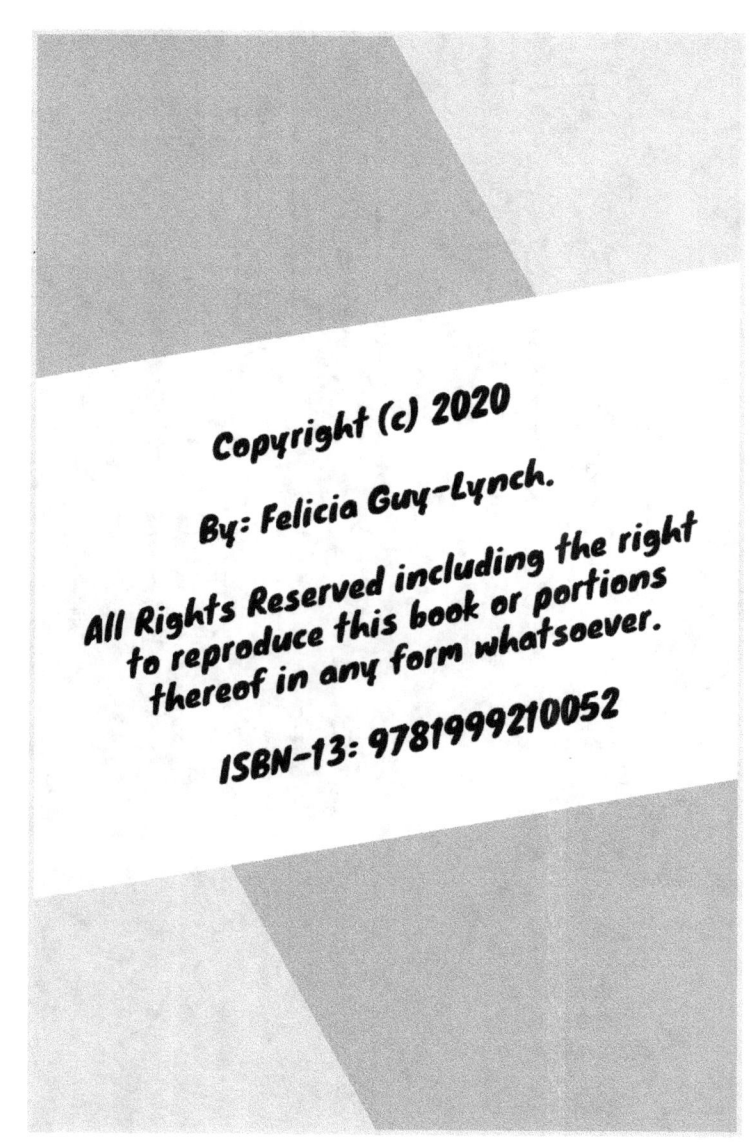

Copyright (c) 2020

By: Felicia Guy-Lynch.

All Rights Reserved including the right to reproduce this book or portions thereof in any form whatsoever.

ISBN-13: 9781999210052

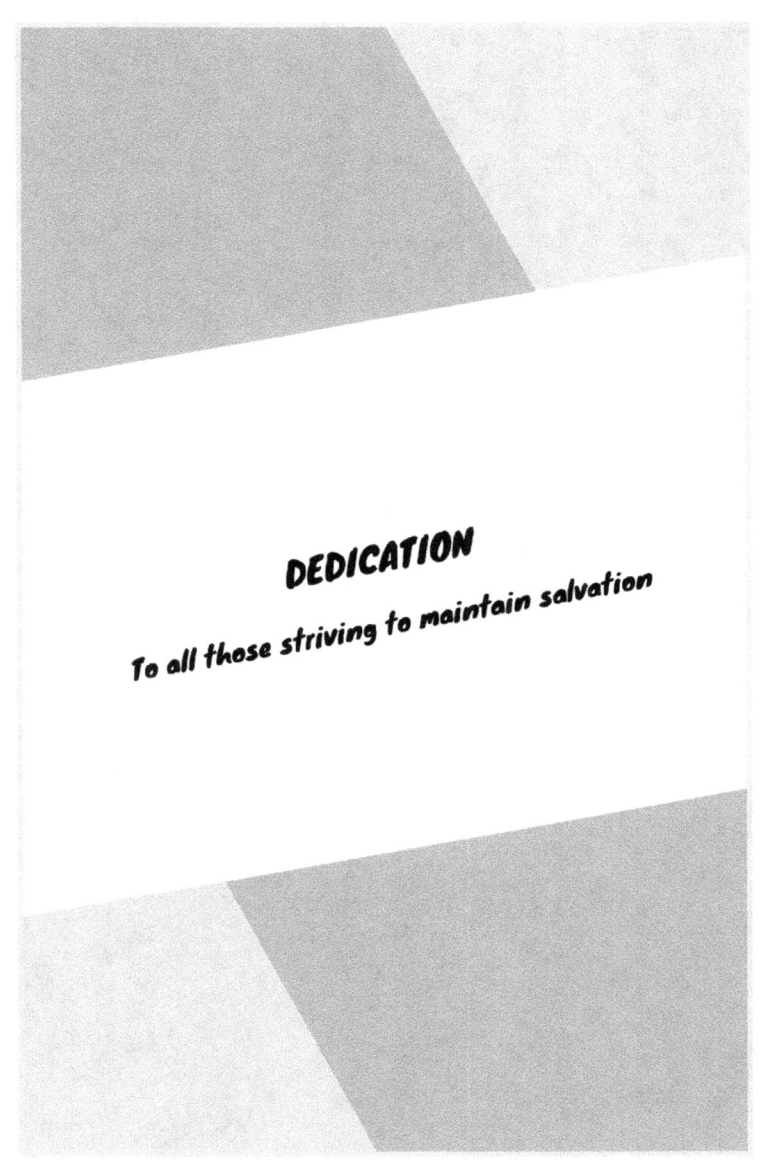

DEDICATION

To all those striving to maintain salvation

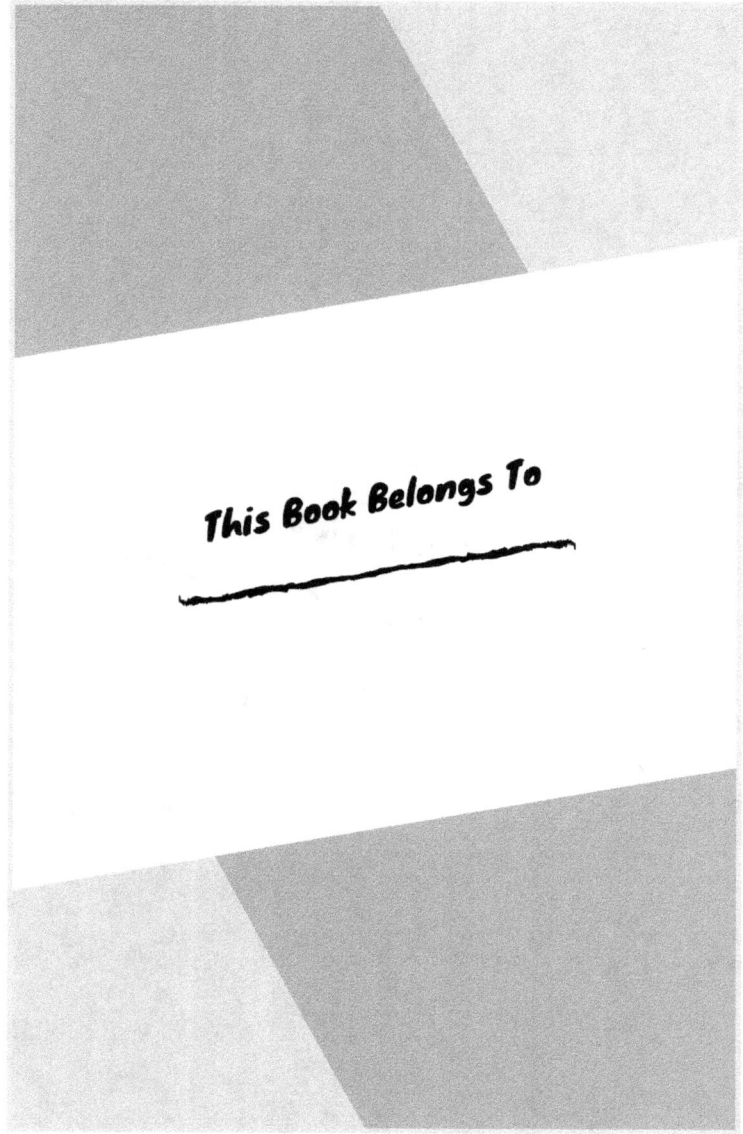

WHAT IS THE ART OF FINDING ISAIAH?

A short story series created by Felicia Guy-Lynch about a young man from Scarborough whose life is full of mix up.

She wanted to create a genuine story that takes place in the Greater Toronto Area (GTA).

THE ART OF FINDING ISAIAH is a coloring book that captures the unfolding of a timeless series. Thank you. Enjoy coloring!

The Art of Finding Isaiah: The Coloring Book

The Art of Finding Isaiah: The Coloring Book

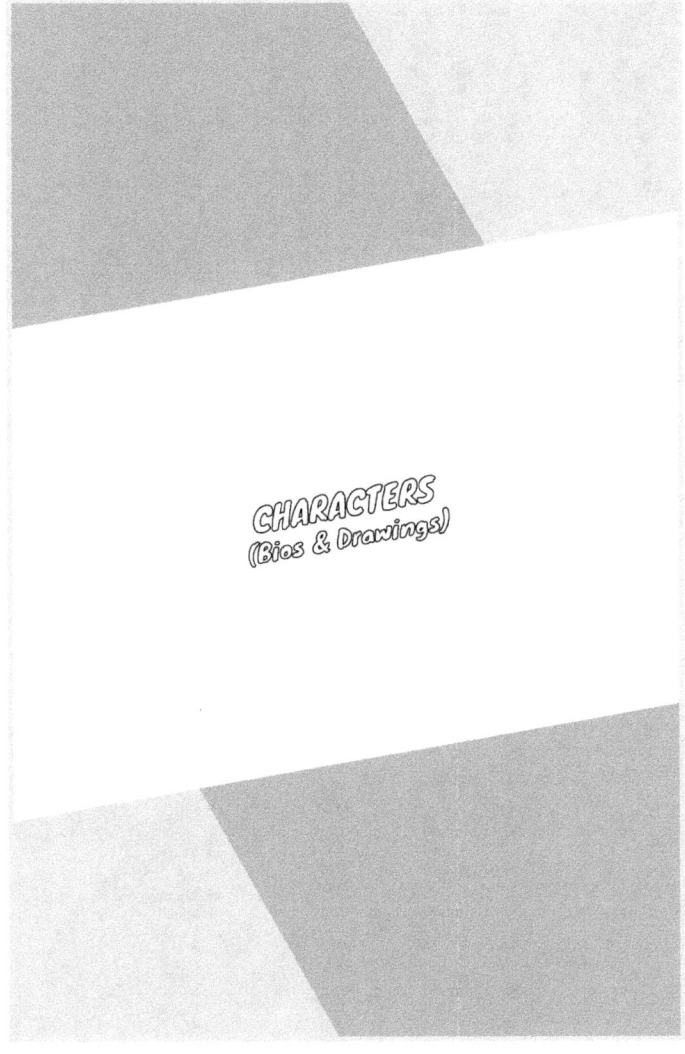

CHARACTERS
(Bios & Drawings)

The Art of Finding Isaiah: The Coloring Book

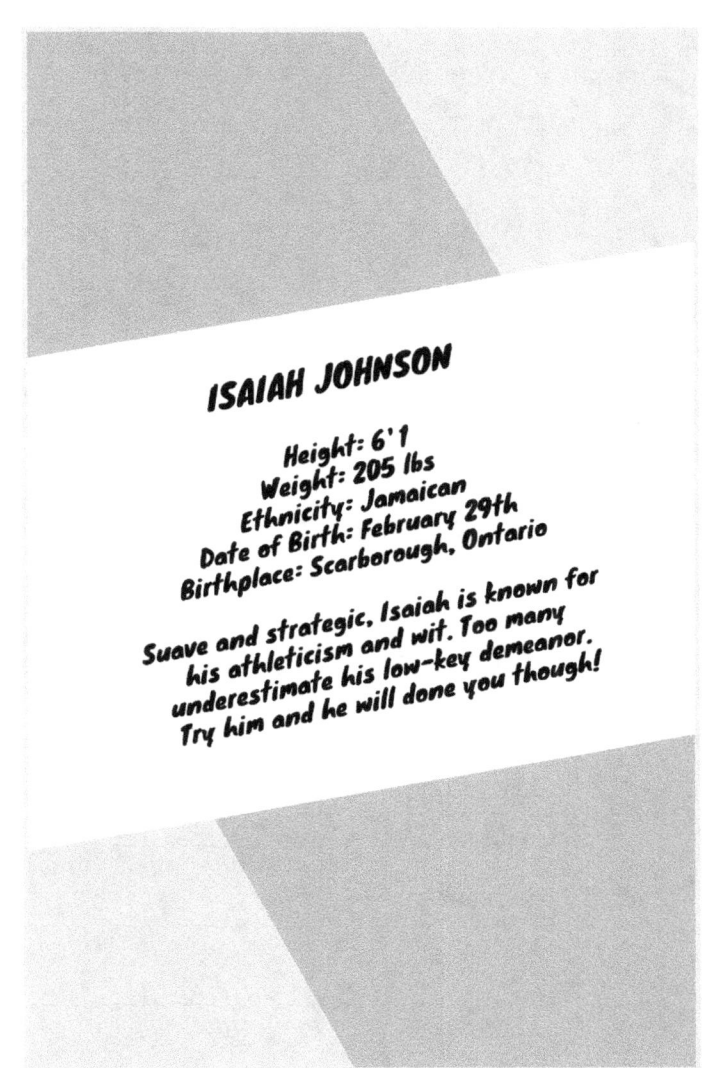

The Art of Finding Isaiah: The Coloring Book

The Art of Finding Isaiah: The Coloring Book

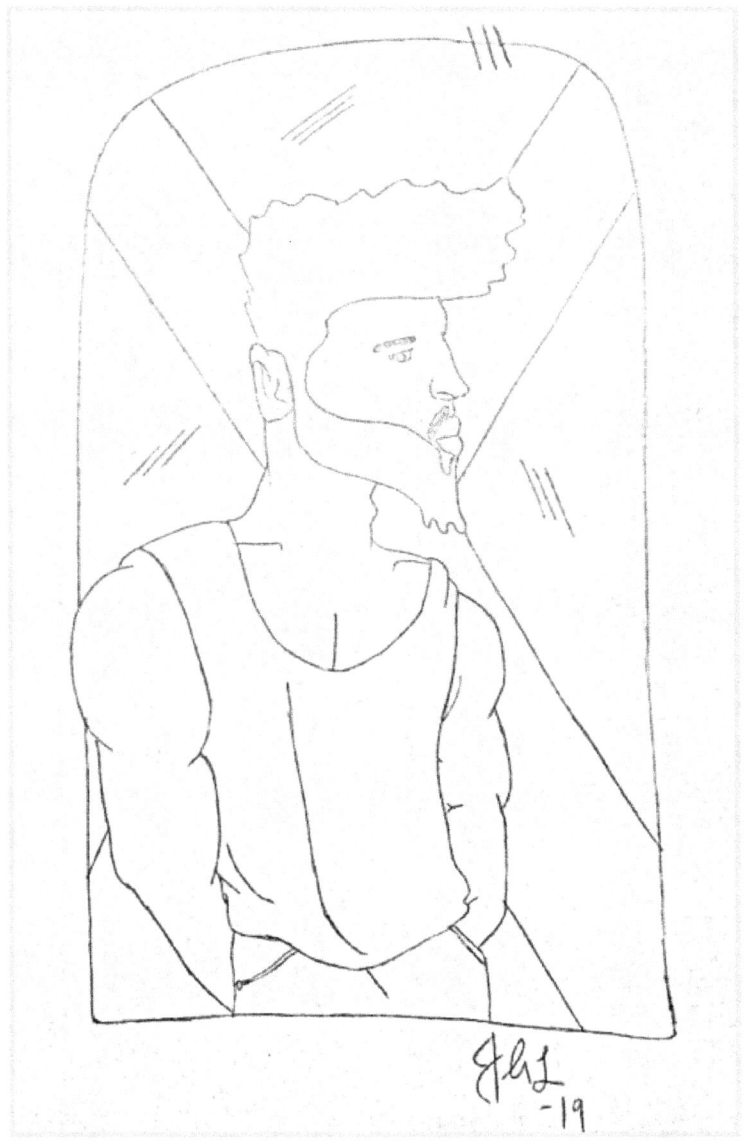

The Art of Finding Isaiah: The Coloring Book

The Art of Finding Isaiah: The Coloring Book

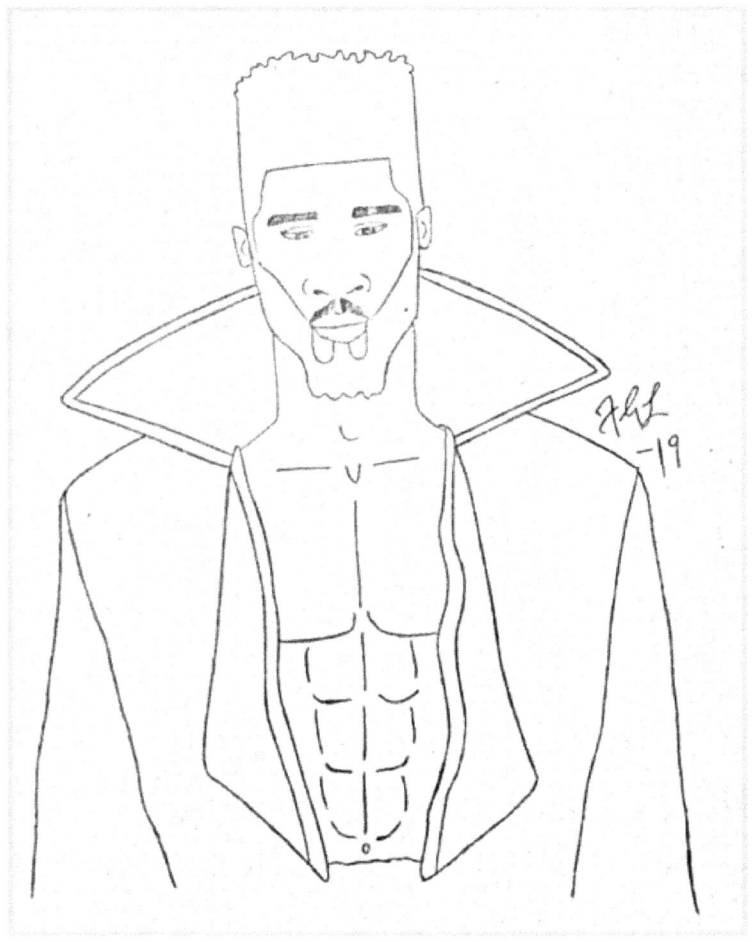

The Art of Finding Isaiah: The Coloring Book

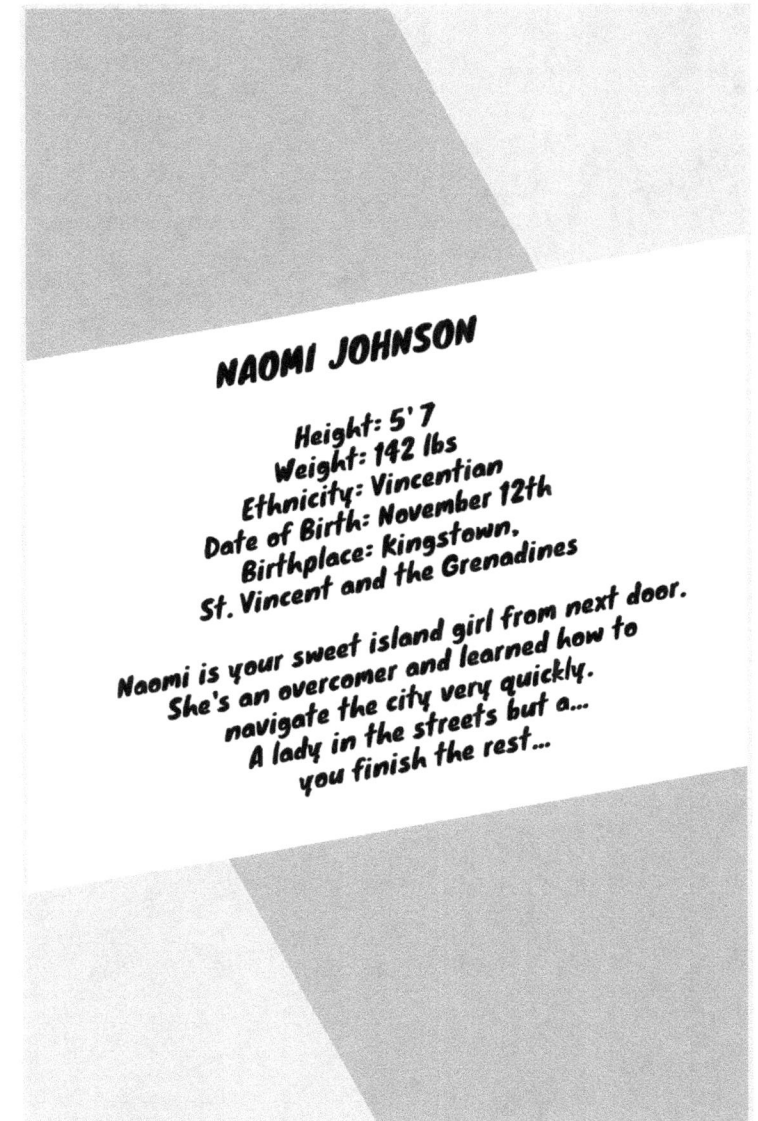

The Art of Finding Isaiah: The Coloring Book

The Art of Finding Isaiah: The Coloring Book

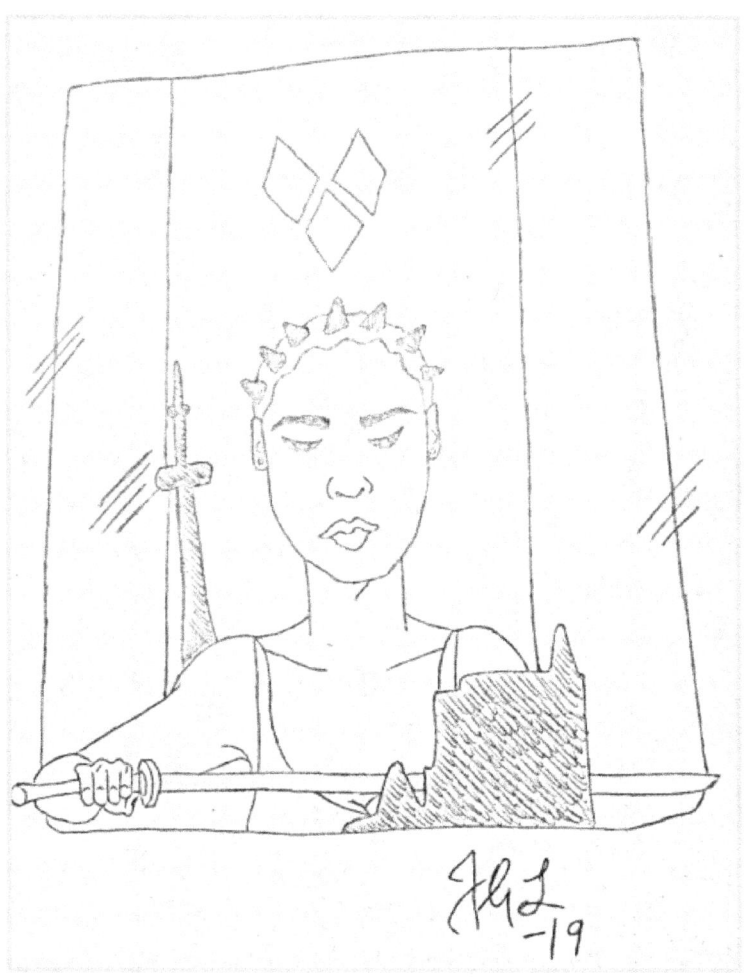

The Art of Finding Isaiah: The Coloring Book

The Art of Finding Isaiah: The Coloring Book

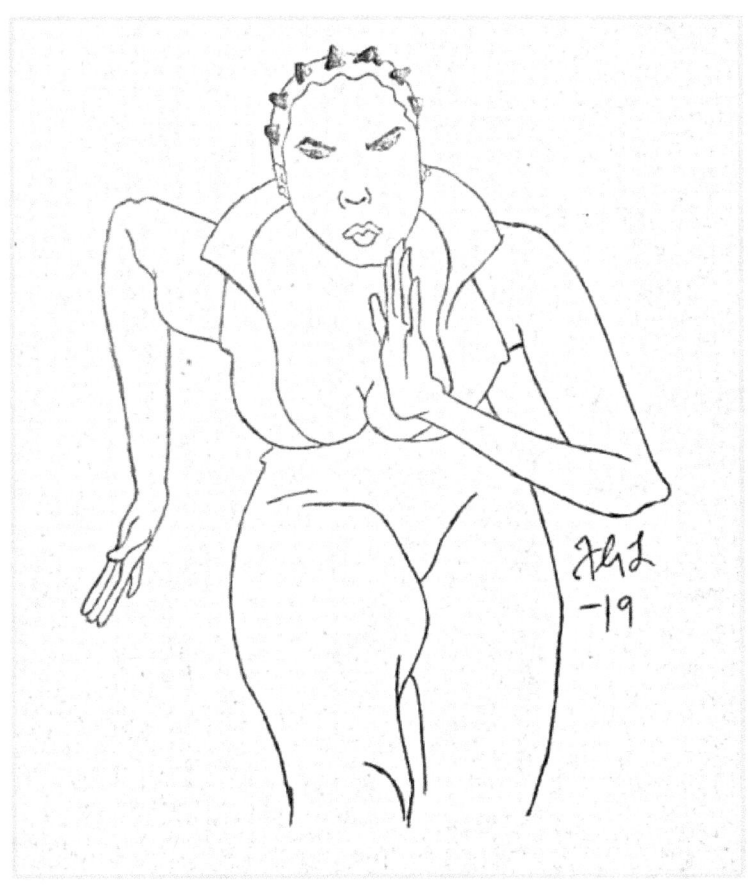

The Art of Finding Isaiah: The Coloring Book

The Art of Finding Isaiah: The Coloring Book

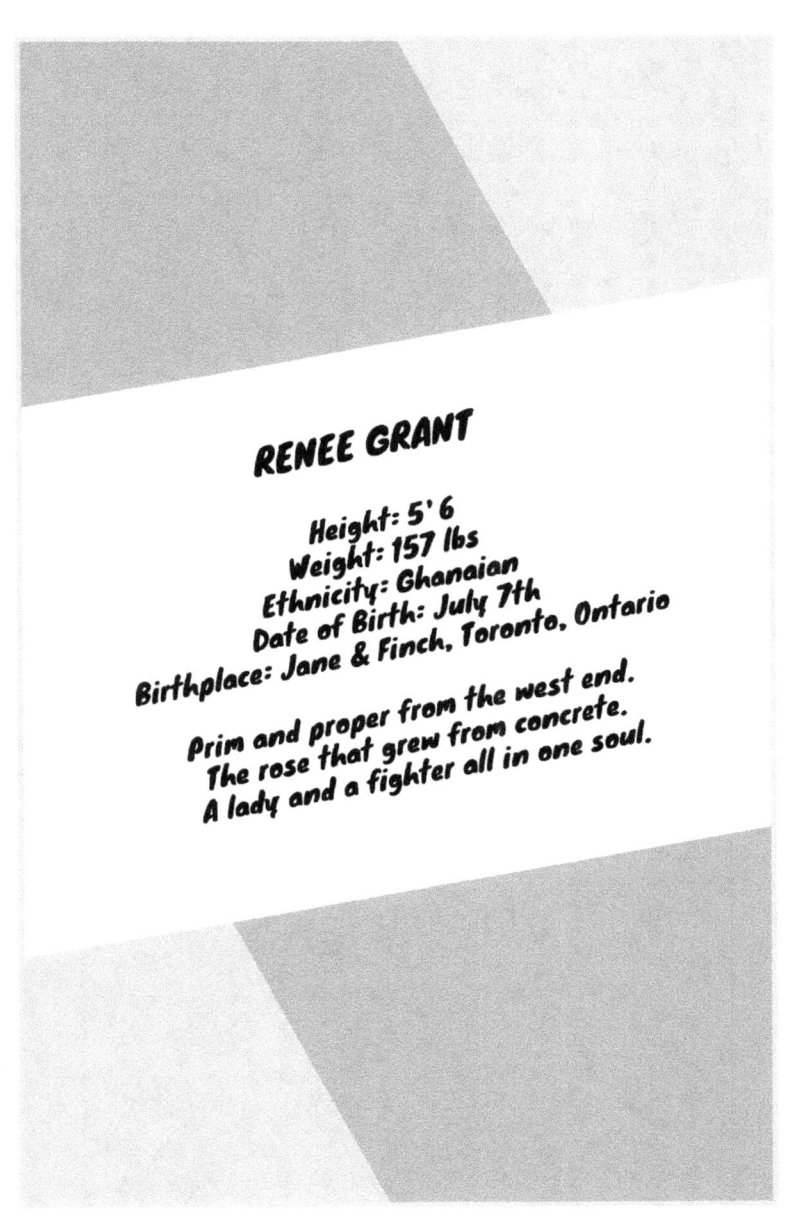

RENEE GRANT

Height: 5'6
Weight: 157 lbs
Ethnicity: Ghanaian
Date of Birth: July 7th
Birthplace: Jane & Finch, Toronto, Ontario

Prim and proper from the west end.
The rose that grew from concrete.
A lady and a fighter all in one soul.

The Art of Finding Isaiah: The Coloring Book

The Art of Finding Isaiah: The Coloring Book

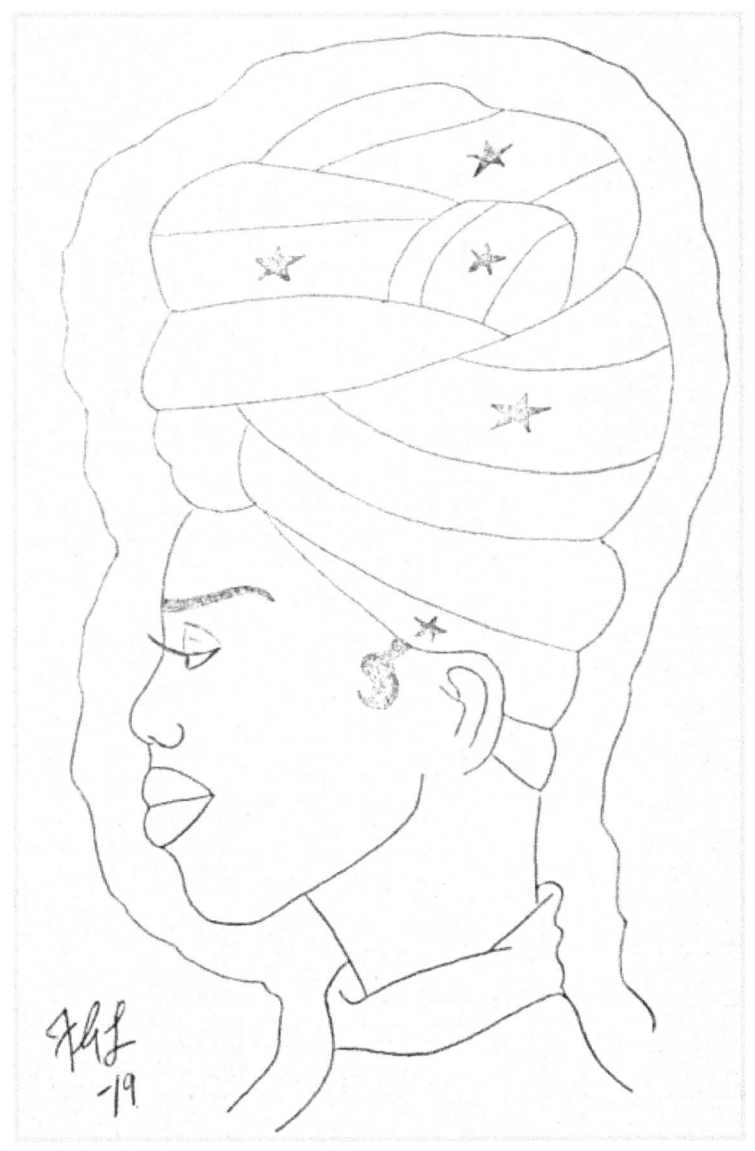

The Art of Finding Isaiah: The Coloring Book

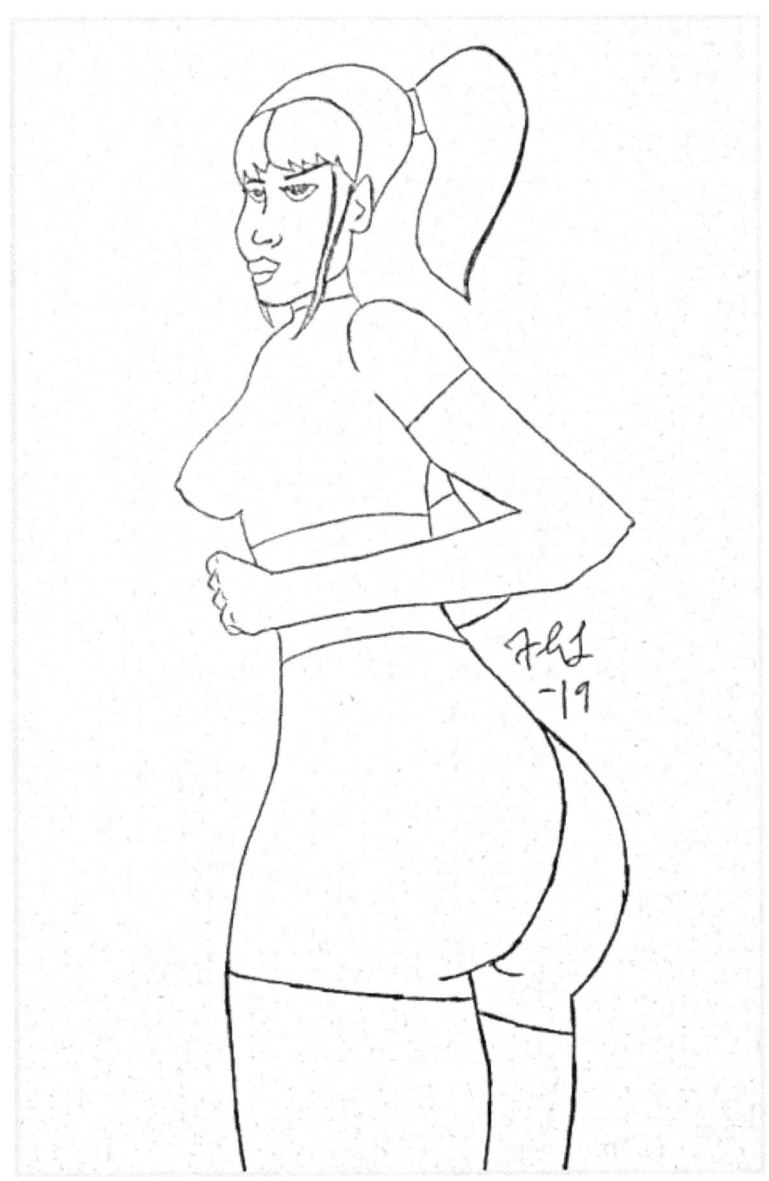

The Art of Finding Isaiah: The Coloring Book

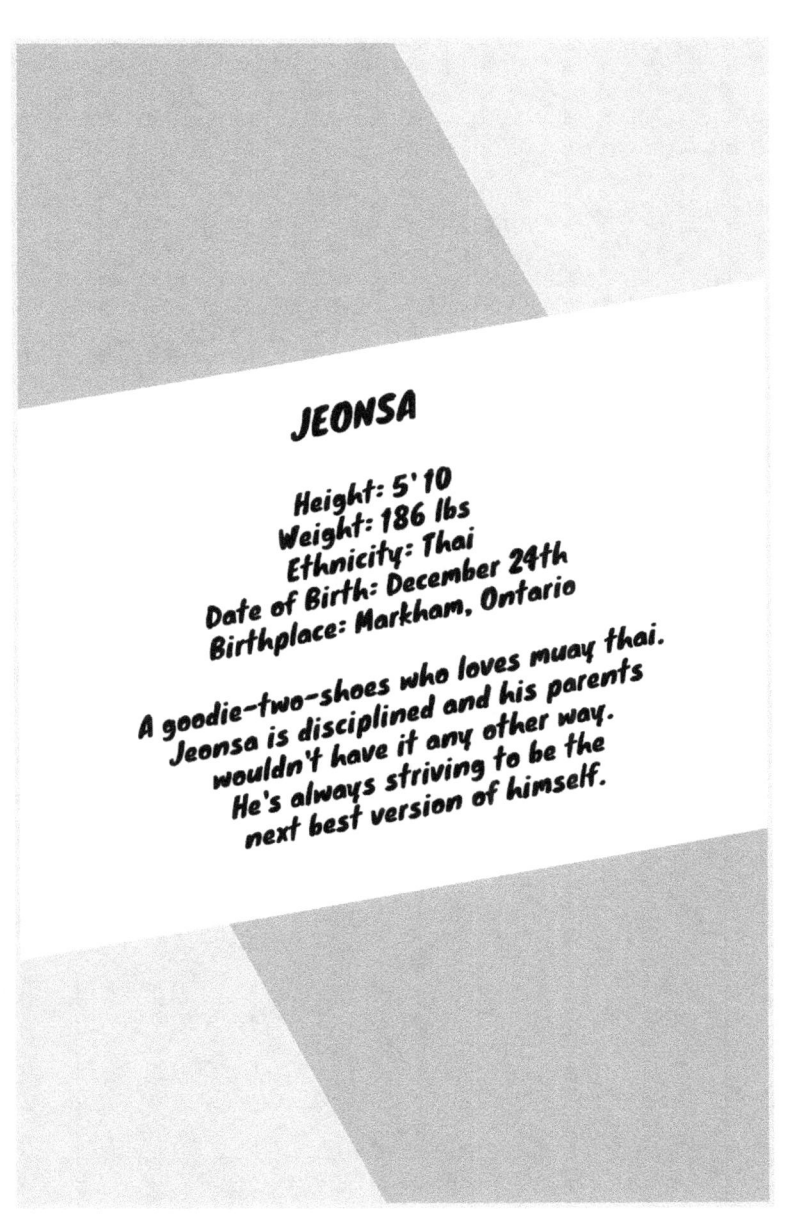

The Art of Finding Isaiah: The Coloring Book

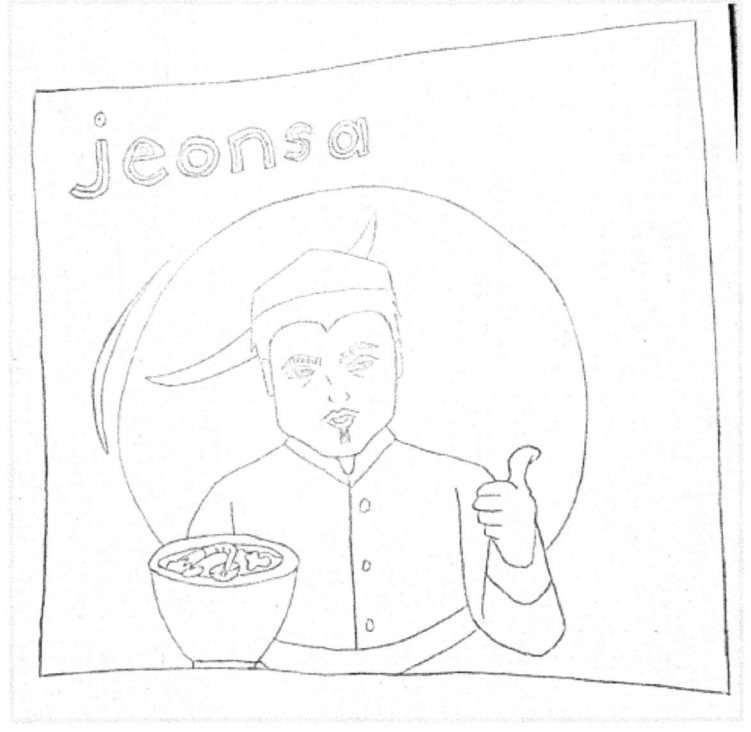

The Art of Finding Isaiah: The Coloring Book

The Art of Finding Isaiah: The Coloring Book

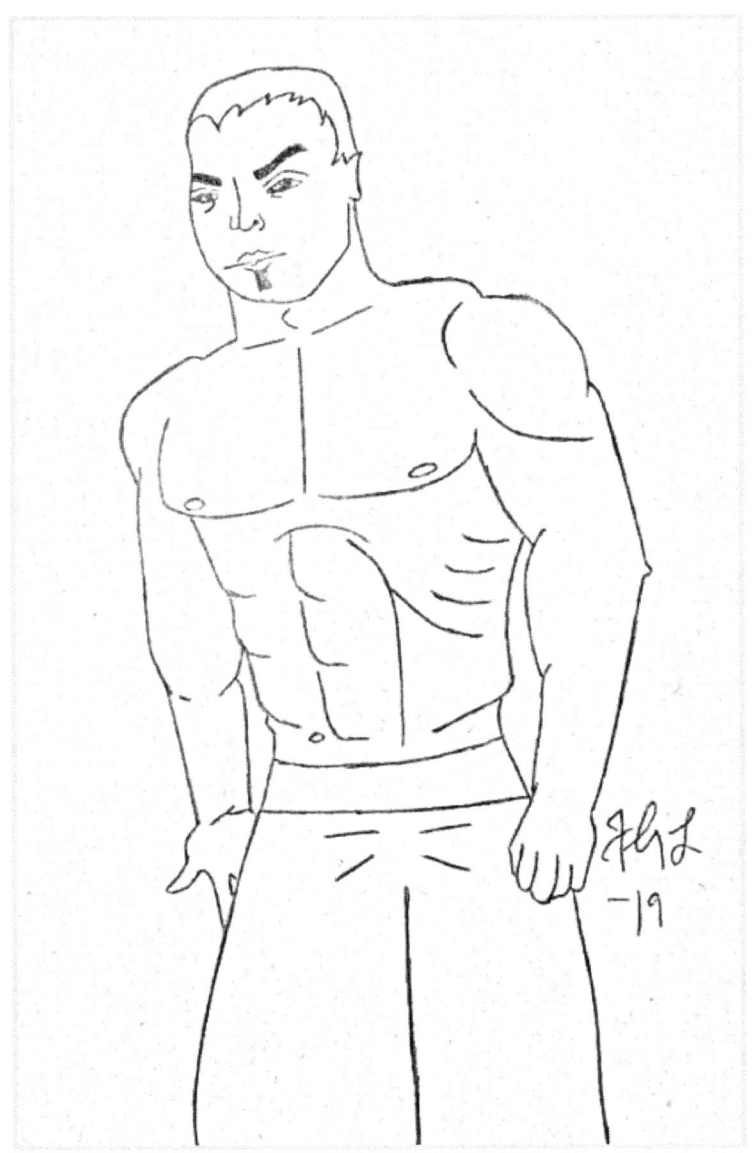

The Art of Finding Isaiah: The Coloring Book

The Art of Finding Isaiah: The Coloring Book

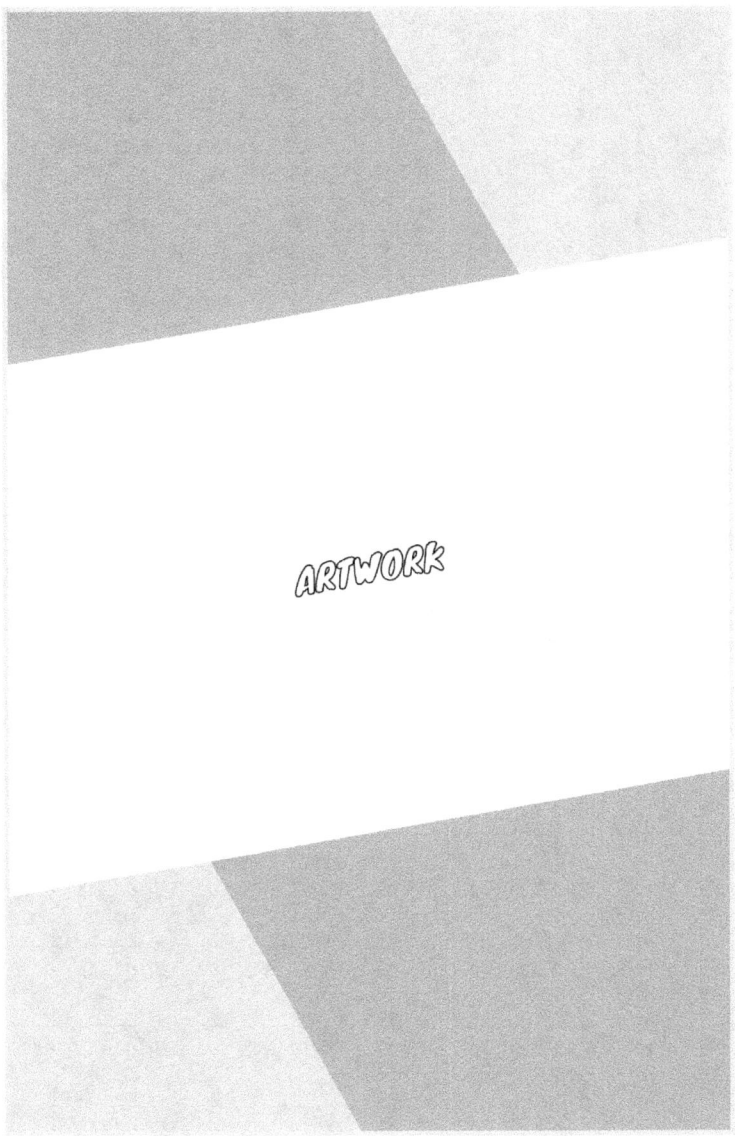

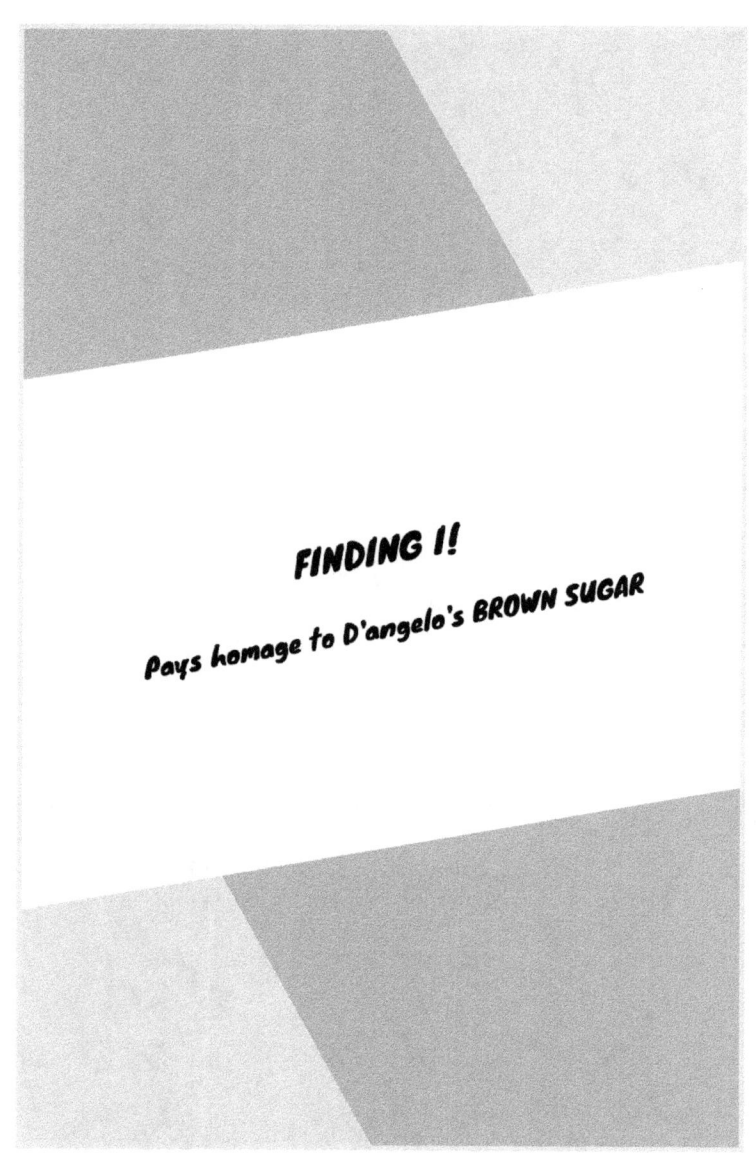

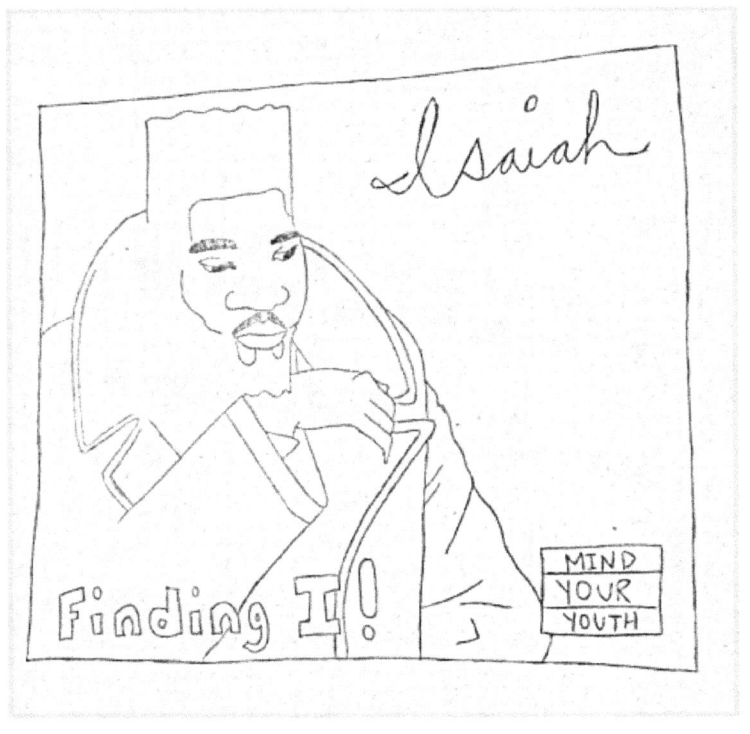

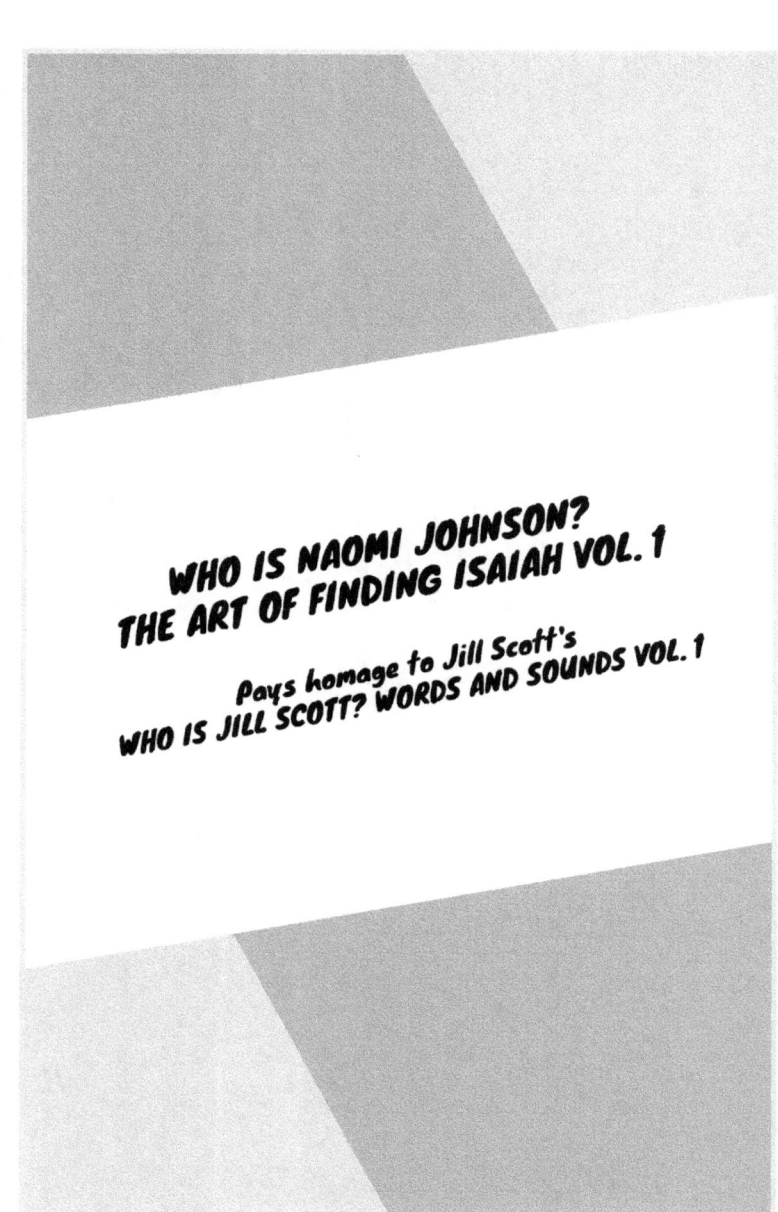

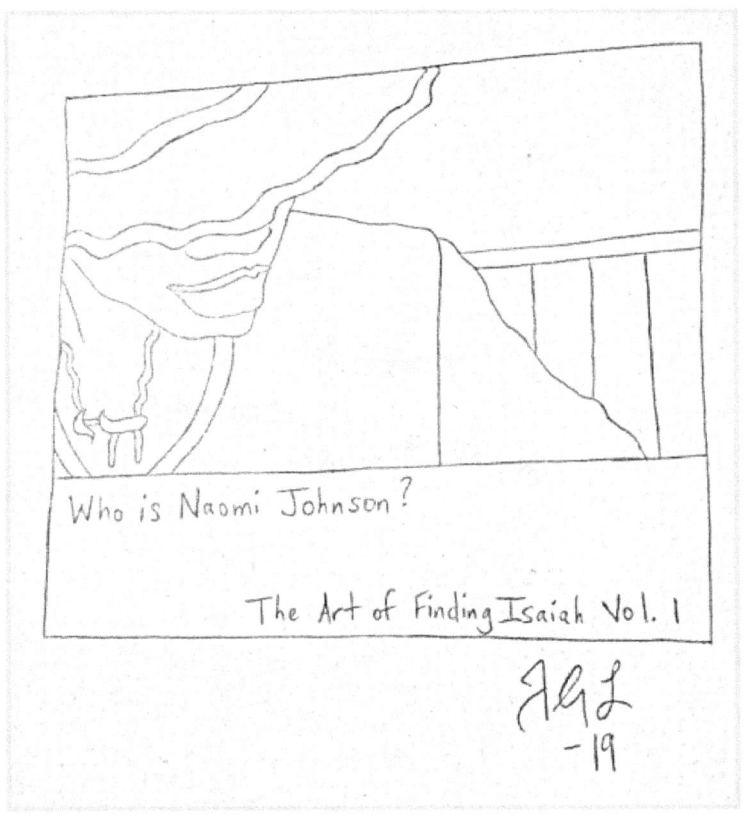

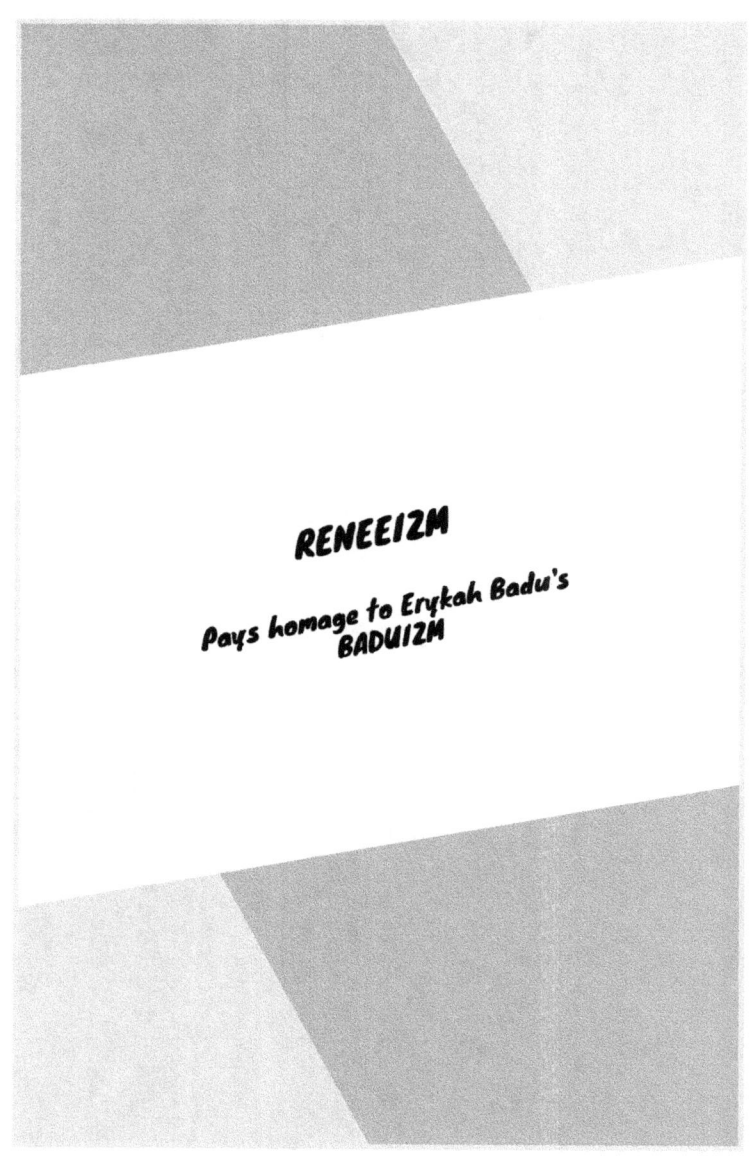

The Art of Finding Isaiah: The Coloring Book

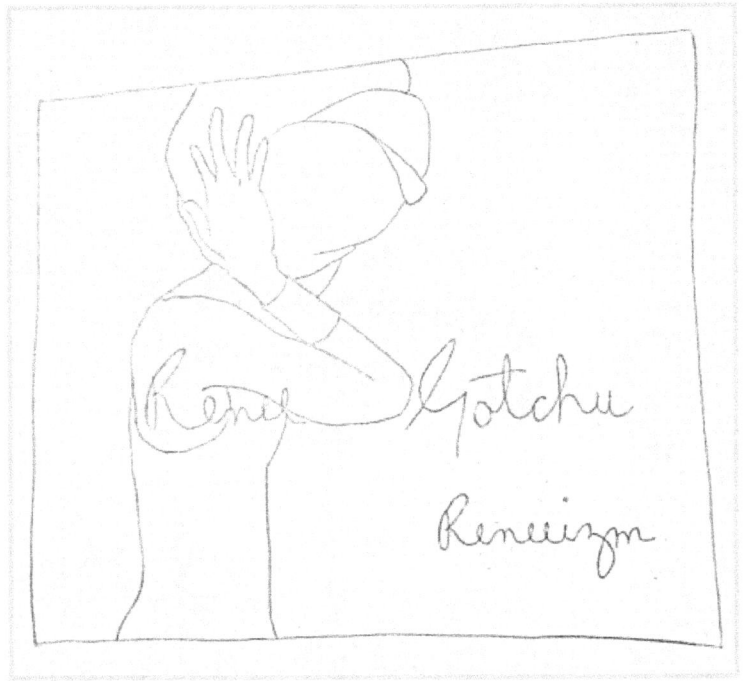

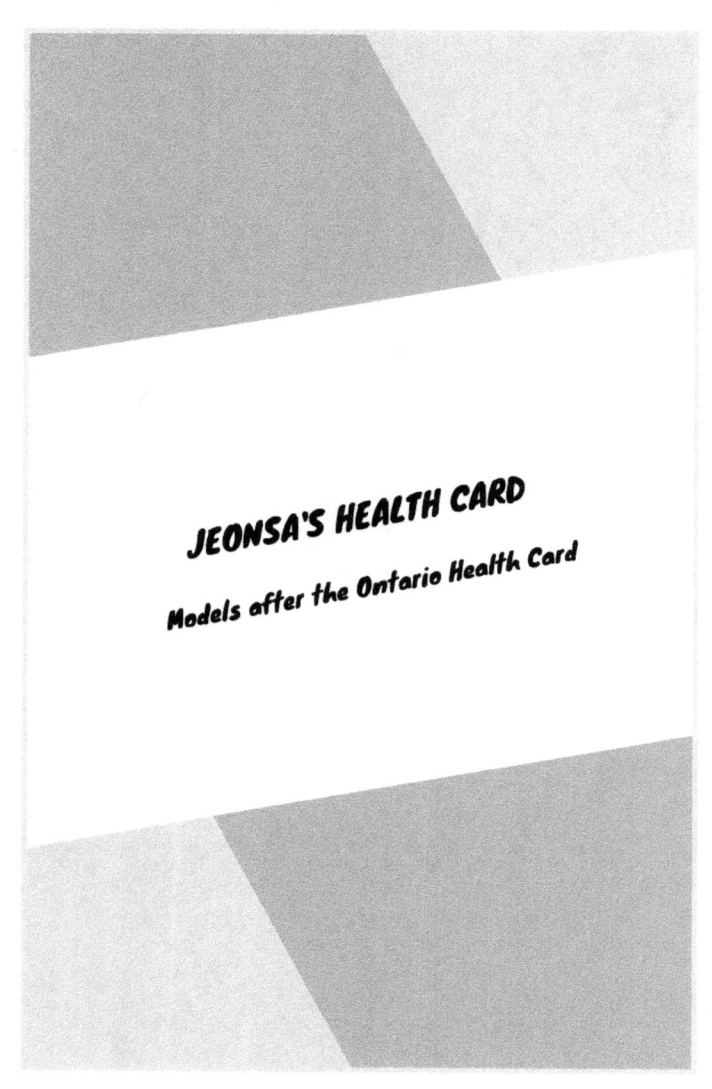

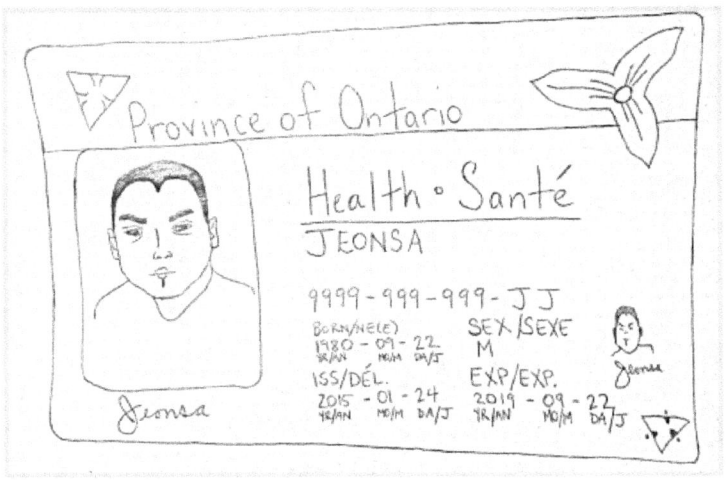

The Art of Finding Isaiah: The Coloring Book

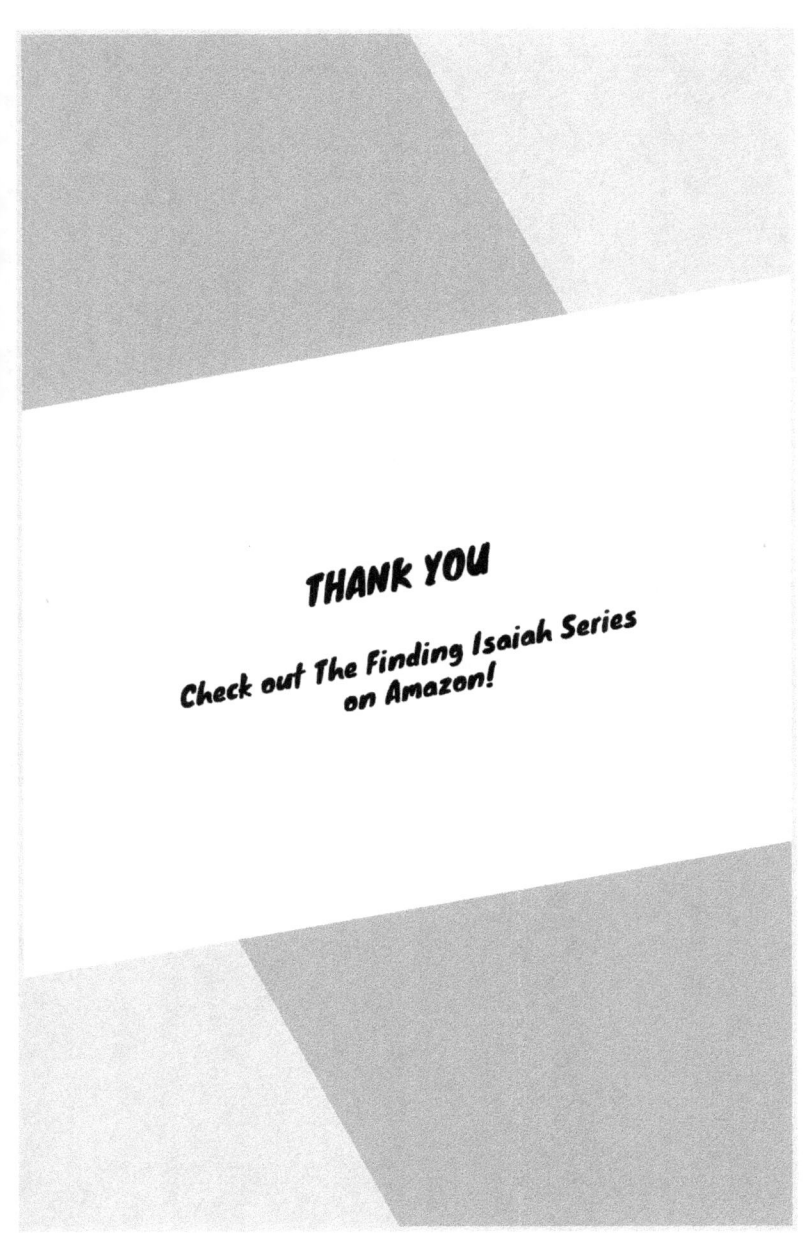

www.ingramcontent.com/pod-product-compliance
Lightning Source LLC
Chambersburg PA
CBHW070951220526
45471CB00007B/2991